FRENCH
CUISINE WITH

Tea

Mariage Frères

Photography Yves Bagros

Styling Laurence du Tilly

Hachette

Contents

Tea from its origins

In the same way that cocoa was given to man by the snake-god Quetzalcoatl, and just like the vine – the work of Osiris or Dionysus –, tea is of heavenly descent. Legend has it that it was created one day in 2737BC, by Chen Nung, the last of China's three mythic emperors. While this divine ruler was relaxing in the gentle shade of a wild tea bush, he boiled a little water to quench his thirst. Three leaves, it is said, fell into his cup: curious, Chen Nung tasted this infusion and found it exquisite. Tea was born.

From the IVth century AD, tea started to become a widespread drink in China, prepared by various methods according to the prevailing fashions under the Tang, Song and then Ming dynasties. Thus were the classic tea preparation techniques defined: boiling, then compression into a block; pounding to reduce it to a powder; and finally infusion, for which the leaves are used.

From its indigenous region, tea spread little by little, appearing in Korea, Tibet, Japan (where a Buddhist monk, Saïcho, introduced it in the IXth century), before conquering, thanks to the caravan routes, all the Mongol lands, Persia, the Muslim world and Russia.

The West discovers tea

Celebrated in the Far East, tea meanwhile remained unknown in the West until almost the middle of the XVIIth century. The Dutch, by whom the East India Company had been founded in 1602, were the first to transport tea to Europe; they were followed by the French and then the English.

In France, Louis XIV was one of the first enthusiasts for this novelty: he asked his doctors

5

to prescribe him tea "to ease his digestion". Later, on September 1st 1686, the Sun King received, from the ambassador to the King of Siam, "a golden tea boiler" (otherwise known as a teapot), a sumptuous gift which confirmed the regal character of the brew soon adopted by the whole court.

Left hand page:
a tea garden (or plantation) in India, at the beginning of the XXth century.

Opposite, right:
English factory, in India, in the 1920s; dried tea is packed for export.

6

The taste for tea

Until the advent of the Ming dynasty, the tea produced in China was green tea, tea whose tender leaves are dried in the shade, rolled by hand and worked to prevent oxidation. Of greater or lesser value according to the variety, this clear infusion was often characterised by a light and refreshing bitterness.

Until the XVIIth century herbs with acrid and aromatic flavours were strongly favoured in France. So at first the French relished green tea. And as Philippe Sylvestre Dufour noted (in his Treaty of Tea, 1685), it needed to be "bitter and with a mild, pleasant aroma, strongly reminiscent of violets".

However, little by little, bitterness ceased to be such a popular taste. What was then called for was the black (oxidized) tea, beloved of the British, originally with a mild and aromatic flavour, and then, when the Empire was able to extend its colonial power even into the plantations of India and Ceylon, uniformly intense, robust, tannic, even spicy. This graded tea flooded the West under the English banner becoming associated with breakfast or afternoon tea and served with stewed fruit, scones, crumpets, toast or cakes. In short, the Europeans simultaneously discovered a taste for both sweets and black tea, whose full-bodied, strong, astringent, and well-rounded liquor went so well with the sugary flavours, whilst the amber or copper-coloured infusion recalled

Nevertheless a puzzle remained: for some, tea was a potion or an unguent, for others a salad leaf, or even a plant for smoking "in the manner of tobacco". But Madame de Sévigné had already appreciated the best part to take from this exotic plant, and it is as the owner of a keen palate that she gives some advice on infusion: "Take a pint of water and bring it to the boil.

Then add half a gros of tea, or two pinches, and remove from the fire, for it does not need to boil. Let it rest like this and steep for the time of two or three paternosters, then serve with fine sugar, in porcelain".

Above: The Treaty of Tea by Philippe Sylvestre Dufour, the first work in French about tea to appear, in 1685.

Right hand page: European traders buying tea in Canton, XVIIIth century, V&A Museum.

8

the warm glow of our western drinks: wines or beers. At the dawn of the XIXth century, these taste associations are confirmed by Grimod de la Reynière: «It is accepted now in Paris that tea can not be served without a dozen plates of dainty pastries. Ladies, young people and children fall upon them greedily, and these sweets appeal to all ages, accommodate all tastes and delight all stomachs".

But beyond a gathering of sweet-lovers, it was also the social occasion that was looked for. For tea became the pretext for elegant outings or receptions: «Teas were given, a quite extraordinary comessation (a light meal) at which, since they were served to people who had already dined well, and there was assumed to be neither appetite nor thirst, the aim was only entertainment and a basis for sweets". Indeed at the beginning of the XXth century and while Anglomania was at its height, five o'clock teas and tea dances were all the rage in France. These social gatherings really took off in luxury seaside hotels (like the Grand Hotel in Cabourg, immortalised by Proust), casinos and restaurants.

But people also entertained at home. Tea, then, was prepared in front of the guests, and the mistress of the house had all the accoutrements at hand: cups, saucers, sugar bowl, plates, embroidered napkins, milk jug, everything to enjoy this pleasant interlude which brought a little relaxation to the strictures of mealtimes. Following these fashions and domestic practices – and unlike in England where tea was drunk from one end of the social scale to the other – in France this drink remained enduringly associated with the bourgeoisie, with privilege and with an old-fashioned image of feminine virtue.

Opposite: Old label and, at the bottom, the «Mariage Frères» trademark.

Right hand page: Modern labels for packaging Mariage Frères' iced teas.

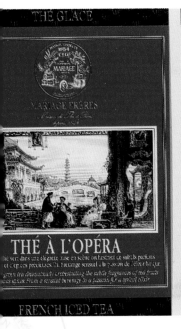

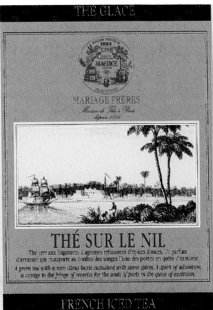

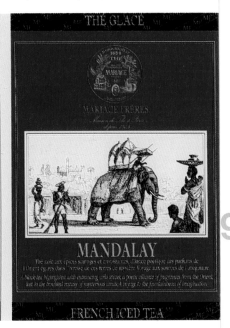

The 1970s:
a garden in the cup

Everything began to change in the 1970s. This was effectively the time when many French people started to learn about teas by enjoying the fruity or floral "blends" which were then in fashion. The addition of berries, spices, vanilla, honey, nuts, citrus fruits and even tropical fruits certainly paved the way for a large majority to discover and to sweeten certain aromas and flavours (notably the astringency and fresh herb taste of Japanese green teas).

But if the craze for these "blends" often gave rise to an improvement…sometimes it resulted in something worse. What was almost forgotten was that the preparation of these teas depended on an extremely ancient and subtle art, which required as much knowledge as imagination. This artistry, originating in China, is in fact comparable to that of the perfumier. While the latter plays with fragrances, the tea taster himself commits to memory the innumerable individual aromas and flavours attached to each garden (plantation), even to each crop. In addition, he also needs to memorise the numerous notes and nuances of essential oils naturally found in leaves, peel, flowers, spices, herbs, seeds, roots or fruits. All that remains is to make beautiful harmonies and to develop clever combinations, the recipes for which are closely-guarded manufacturing secrets. The cup, then, becomes a garden of flowers or fruits.

10

The French tea tradition

In the vast world of tea, the French very soon showed their originality. Isn't it said that it was a Frenchwoman, Madame de la Sablière, who – in the XVIIth century – first had the idea of adding milk to her tea? A French touch which was going to drive the English crazy. Yet this curiosity, this instinctive inventiveness is found among professional tasters. Here the amazing descendants of the Mariages, very early specialist merchants in "overseas trade", had significant influence.

From 1660, Nicolas Mariage made many trips to the East Indies then to the India of the Mogul Emperors, and was chosen to be part of a royal delegation charged with signing a trade agreement with the Shah of Persia. At the same time, his brother Pierre was sailing towards Madagascar as special envoy of the East India Company. A century later, Jean-François Mariage, living in Lille, was already trading in teas, spices and colonial goods, and training his four sons.

On June 1st 1854 in Paris, his descendants, Édouard and Henri, founded the company which today still bears their name.

The Mariages are thus found perpetually at the heart of the tea trade. Methodical, inquisitive and daring, in the 1980s they were the first to open their range of special blends to individuals, teaching them the subtleties of region and year of growth and of harvesting, explaining the various ways of fermentation, improving the quality of the tea leaf to gourmet standard, and initiating them into the subtleties of preparation. Right then French tea was crying out for a new image with neither social nor taste prejudices. So enthusiasts (from all backgrounds) discovered a universe teeming with undreamt-of pleasures: the almond taste of Darjeeling teas harvested in spring; the blackcurrant notes in certain Indian teas; the flavour of sweet chestnut in the semi-oxidized Formosa teas; the smoothness of green teas from China, or the freshness of Japanese green teas… an inexhaustible palette of little gourmet pleasures.

Opposite: caddies used in the past by Mariage Frères tasters to present their teas to their clients including, for example, the royal court of Belgium.

Right hand page: jasmine tea, chrysanthemum tea, or as here, fresh mint tea… tea travels from civilisation to civilisation.

12

Opposite: tea and sweet
tastes go well together;
by 1860 the Mariage brothers
had already invented tea-
flavoured chocolate, calling
it "chocolate of the Mandarins".

Cooking with tea

Towards the middle of the XVIIth century, recipes
making use of carefully-crafted techniques
appeared in France for the first time.

From then on this spirit of organisation became
the hallmark of French classical cookery, whose
great reform movement of which favoured
simplicity and the search for the best produce,
and which organised the meal around the
progression of flavours.

Everything was associated with a real appetite
for novelty, even exoticism. Henceforth, tea could
appear as a possible, even exceptional, ingredient
thanks to its varied flavours and the diversity of its

forms (as leaves, broken, powdered, etc). Indeed,
from 1742, La Chapelle included a recipe
for "cream of tea" in his 'Cuisinier moderne'
cookbook. But two centuries later, no further
progress had been made: the XIXth century
Larousse encyclopaedia mentioned this cream
as the only possible use of tea in cookery!
It was not until the French culinary arts and the
tea tasters met that this "ingredient" revealed all
its gastronomic potential. And thus, for almost
two decades, day after day, the Mariage Frères
chefs in their Parisian restaurants have been
offering original and exclusive recipes for fish,
seafood, poultry, pastries or ice creams with a tea
base. The palette of aromas, tastes, colours
and textures is of an undreamt-of range. Here
for the first time are presented a gourmet selection
of them.

Opposite: to overcome
the pitfalls of the Tea
Route, leaves were
compressed into "bricks"
decorated with good
luck symbols.

Left hand page: a drink,
tea is also used for its
relaxing properties; here
a "tea plait" to make an
infusion... for the bath.

13

How about tea as the perfect ingredient for modern
gastronomy? Marrying flavours and perfumes
of flowers, fruits, spices or fresh herbs, it responds
exactly to our desire to find a taste of nature
and authenticity on our plate.
Besides, it's associated with our desire for light yet
tasty cooking. Lastly it satisfies all those – ever more
numerous – for whom the meal is a pretext for little
gourmet journeys: from mint of the East
to Japanese chrysanthemum or from cinnamon
of the Moluccas to Mandarin jasmine. With these
40 tea recipes, you can welcome all the treasures
of the world to your table and skilfully prepare
savoury and sweet dishes, for special occasions
as well as for everyday.

Salad dressing with Matcha Uji tea

Serves 4-6
Preparation time: 5 mins
2½ tsp powdered Matcha Uji green tea
(box page 20)
1 pinch each pepper and salt
1 tbs mustard (optional)
5 cl white vinegar
5 cl rice vinegar (from an Asian grocer)
25 cl sunflower oil
Equipment: 1 salad bowl; 1 whisk

16

■ In a salad bowl, combine the salt, pepper and mustard (if used).

■ Add the Matcha tea powder and blend well using the whisk.

■ Next gradually add the vinegars and finally the oil, drop by drop, taking care to keep whisking vigorously.

■ *There are many methods of preparing tea salad dressings. In the case of the salad dressing with Matcha tea, the tea powder is added as a spice. But the tea leaves can also be steeped in hot or cold vinegar.*

■ *For the Métis-Thé rouge dressing (box page 68), for example, infuse 5 tsp of tea leaves in 15 cl of cold raspberry vinegar for 12 hours. Then strain, add salt and pepper and whisk vigorously with 20 cl of sunflower oil.*

■ *For the black, smoked Tarry Souchong tea dressing (boxes pages 30 and 36), reduce 10 cl of sherry vinegar and 5 cl of balsamic vinegar in a saucepan; then add salt, pepper and 5 tsp of tea leaves. Allow to infuse, turn up the heat while whisking in 20 cl of sunflower oil and finally strain.*

■ *These two recipes are designed for 4-6 people.*

Salad with Taïping Houkui tea leaves

Serves 8
Preparation time: 10 mins
Humidification of the tea leaves:
12 hrs in the refrigerator
10 tsp Taïping Houkui tea leaves
(box opposite)
1 head lollo rossa lettuce
1 head frisée
1 head oak-leaf lettuce
1 head radicchio
For the dressing:
3 cl soy sauce
10 cl sesame oil
Equipment: 3 salad bowls (1 large and 2 small);
1 fine tea strainer; 1 whisk

■ The night before, soak the tea leaves in cold water (allow four times their volume of water, e.g. 4 cups water to one of tea), in a small salad bowl, taking care to mix in the tea well. Put the bowl in the refrigerator for at least 12 hrs.

■ The next day, mix and wash the lettuces in water to which vinegar has been added, and spin well. Strain the tea leaves through the tea strainer without squeezing. Combine the lettuce and tea leaves and drain again.

■ For the dressing: pour the soy sauce into a small bowl and whisk in the sesame oil.
■ Place the tea leaf salad in the large salad bowl, drizzle with dressing, mix and serve immediately. Serving suggestion: trying adding warm, seared langoustines or steamed fish.

■ *Green tea's different qualities can be distinguished from one another by their colour, general appearance, and aroma. Taïping Houkui is a green (that is non-oxidized) China tea with large, dark, shiny, downy green leaves. These give a clear infusion and the most delicate taste. On the plate, their perfume of orchids and their highly developed flavour go well with the crunch of the lettuce and the salty-acidic flavours of the sauce. If this tea from the province of Anhui is not available, try a tender spring-crop green tea.*

18

Salmon and green tea dressing

Serves 4

Preparation time: 10 mins

Refrigeration: 4 hrs

400 g skinless, boneless salmon fillet

200 g soba noodles (Japanese pasta, from an Asian grocer)

a few drops sesame oil

Matcha Uji green tea salad dressing

(page 16 and box opposite)

salt and freshly ground pepper

Equipment: *1 large non-stick frying pan; 1 large dish;*

1 large saucepan; 1 sieve; kitchen paper and cling film

■ Wash the fish and dry carefully. Heat the frying pan; sear the salmon fillet for about 30 secs on each side. Season both sides during cooking. Place in the large dish, cover with cling film and keep cool for 4 hrs.

■ Bring to the boil a large saucepan of water, add the noodles and cook for about 2 mins after they come back to the boil. Drain and plunge into iced water. Then drain again and add a little sesame oil to prevent sticking.

■ When the salmon is cold, slice it into fine strips. Divide the noodles between the plates, arrange the strips of salmon in rosettes and served accompanied by the Matcha Uji green tea dressing.

■ *Matcha ("tea powder") is a Japanese green tea whose leaves, dried then chopped into small pieces, are stone-ground to reduce them to powder. Used in the tea ceremony, Matcha provides a powerful and intense drink, a tonic and digestive, rich in vitamin C and lightly caffeinated, which can be drunk hot or iced. This tea, which goes extremely well with all sorts of dishes, is available in specialist shops. However, note that the Uji variety, created from an imperial blend called Gyokuro, is extremely dense and perfumed. Its colour is superb; but, with its powerful aromas, it is advised to use it sparingly, even economically.*

20

Crunchy vegetables and "sesame green tea"

Serves 4
Preparation and cooking time: 30 mins
4 carrot tops
4 stems asparagus
100 g mange tout
200 g Romanesco broccoli
4 baby courgettes
4 baby fennel bulbs
4 baby marrows
100 g shiitake mushrooms (Asian grocers)
100 g soya bean sprouts
4 tbs sesame oil
4 tbs sherry vinegar
4 tbs soy sauce
2 tbs chopped coriander (or parsley)
4 tbs "sesame green tea" (box opposite)
salt, pepper
Equipment: 1 large saucepan; 1 colander; 1 frying pan

■ Cook the vegetables (except the mushrooms and soya sprouts) in boiling water, making sure not to overcook them, chill them in iced water and drain.

■ Brown the mushrooms, soya bean sprouts and then all the other previously-cooked vegetables in the sesame oil, in a hot frying pan; at the last moment, add the vinegar and soy sauce and season.

■ Sprinkle with coriander or parsley and "sesame green tea". Serve immediately.

■ *"Sesame green tea" is a ready-made commercial blend – like a condiment – containing Japanese Sencha tea, sesame seeds, seaweed, dried plum, shiso powder (a plant from the mint family, often used in Japanese cookery), salt and sugar. As it is, it can be used to flavour salads, crudités, vegetables, soups, pasta, gratins, eggs, etc., giving a taste at once fresh, iodised and nutty.*

■ *This preparation can be replaced with your own mix of grilled sesame seeds, salt and young, green tea (ask for spring crop), in broken leaves.*

Monkey King asparagus

Serves 4

Preparation time: 25 mins

Cooking time: 5 mins for the asparagus

20 mins for the sauce

2 bunches green asparagus

For the hollandaise sauce:

200 g butter

4 tsp Monkey King tea leaves

(box opposite)

4 egg yolks

5 cl single cream

juice of ½ lemon

salt, pepper

Equipment: 3 saucepans (1 large, 1 medium, and 1 small); 1 whisk; 1 fine sieve

■ Bring the water to the boil in the large saucepan. Clean and peel the asparagus and drop them into the boiling water (they will be ready about 1 min after they come back to the boil). Then plunge them into iced water.

■ For the hollandaise sauce, first clarify the butter: melt it over a gentle heat; then skim off the foam and collect the pure butter, leaving the milk at the bottom of the pan. Heat the clarified butter in the medium saucepan, and add the tea, allowing it to infuse for 3 minutes, whisking constantly. Strain and keep hot.

■ Put the egg yolks into the small saucepan with 2 tbs of cold water. Whisk over a gentle heat until the mixture foams, like a zabaglione. Remove from the heat. Add salt and pepper and beat in the clarified butter little by little; add the cream and the lemon juice. Strain and keep hot.

■ Before serving, drop the asparagus back into boiling water and drain well. Serve the sauce on the side.

■ *The Monkey King is a green jasmine tea from the Chinese province of Hunan. The delicate and distinctive taste of jasmine isn't overpowering, and above all doesn't mask the taste of the tea. Other jasmine blend teas could be substituted for Monkey King, but be careful with teas that are too "floral": often the petals or the essences are added at the end of processing; if the smell is very powerful, they quickly go stale and when hot, leave only the base bitterness of the tea.*

24

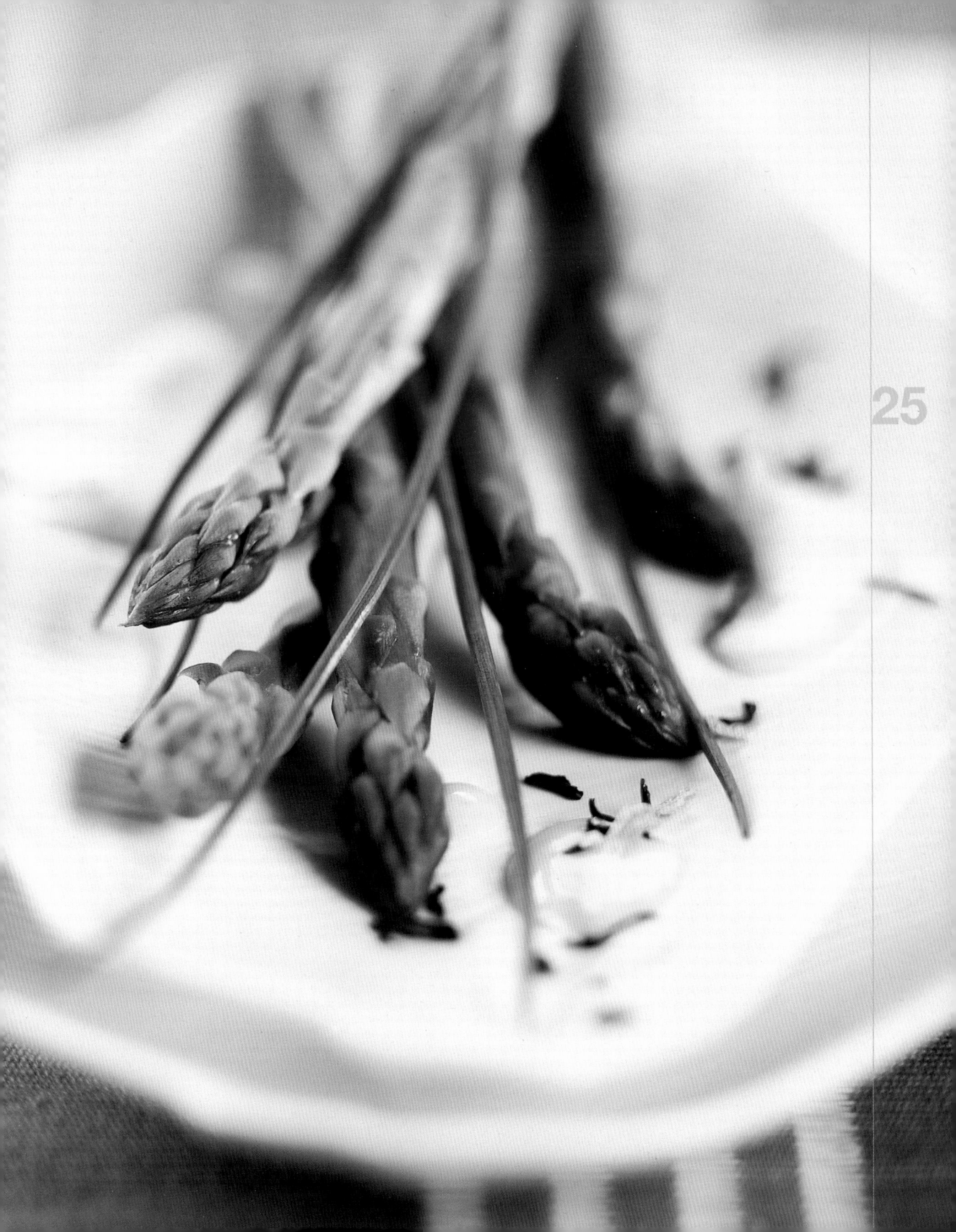

Tzar Alexandre tomato bavarois

Serves 6
Preparation time: 20 mins
Cooking time: 1 hr
Refrigeration: 4 hrs
500 g fresh tomatoes
1 red pepper
1 stick of celery
100 g tomato purée
3 threads of saffron
1 sprig of thyme
2 basil leaves
2 cloves of garlic, chopped
1 tbs sugar
To finish the bavarois:
5 gelatine leaves
100 g double cream
1 tbs ketchup
1 tbs chopped tarragon
1 tsp Tabasco
salt and pepper
For the Tzar Alexandre tea dressing:
3 tbs balsamic vinegar
1 tbs Tzar Alexandre tea leaves
(box opposite)
6 tbs olive oil
salt, pepper
Equipment: 1 large saucepan; 1 blender; 1 fine sieve; 1 bavarois mould

■ Quarter the tomatoes and roughly chop the pepper and celery and put them all in the saucepan with the tomato purée. Then blend and strain.

■ Add the previously softened and strained gelatine, the fresh cream, ketchup, tarragon, Tabasco, salt and pepper to the mixture. Pour this bavarois into the mould and refrigerate for 4 hrs.

■ For the dressing, warm the vinegar, add the tea, leave to infuse for 1 min, add the olive oil, salt and pepper, and mix together.

■ Just before serving, turn the bavarois out of its mould and serve the dressing alongside.

■ *Tzar Alexandre is a "Russian style" tea, that is, one enhanced with bergamot and other citrus fruits; in addition, it is delicately smoked and includes "silver tips" which are the buds of the tea leaf. Lightly smoked or Earl Grey teas can be used instead (boxes pages 30 and 80).*

Little pot of jelly

Serves 8-10
Preparation time: 3 hrs
Humidification of the tea leaves: 12 hrs
Refrigeration: 4-6 hrs
Cooking time: 10 mins
5 tsp Taïping Houkui tea leaves
(box page 18)
1.2 l fish stock
1 bunch flat-leaf parsley
1 sprig thyme
1 bay leaf
1 bunch dill
15 gelatine leaves
Equipment: 1 salad bowl; 1 saucepan; 1 whisk;
1 muslin square; 1 fine sieve; 1 large bowl of ice cubes;
1 wooden spatula; 8-10 small, clear pots

■ The day before, plunge the tea leaves in a bowl of cold water (allow 6 times their volume in water). Toss well and leave to soak for at least 12 hrs.

■ The next day, bring the fish stock to the boil; add the herbs, previously tied in the muslin square, and keep on a low boil for 5 mins, all the while whisking. Remove the herbs and strain.

■ Soften the gelatine in the cold water, drain and add to the stock.

■ Pour the stock onto the ice, stirring all the time (this process will take around 20 mins). Use a wooden spatula rather than a whisk which would form bubbles. When the mixture starts to set, add the tea leaves (previously drained but not squeezed) and spoon into the small, clear pots. Refrigerate for 4-6 hrs. Enjoy cold.

■ *This jelly is delicious enjoyed as it is with canapés. But it is also a tasty accompaniment: with, for example, Green tea parcels (see page 46), or with steamed, buttered vegetables.*

28

Foie gras with Tarry Souchong tea jelly

30

Serves 6
Preparation and cooking time: 1½ hour
Refrigeration: 12 hrs for the terrine;
4-6 hrs for the jelly
1 x 600 g lobe of duck foie gras
20 g salt
1 level tbs caster sugar
freshly ground pepper
For the tea jelly:
5 gelatine leaves
1 pot of Tarry Souchong tea jelly (box opposite)
1 glass of champagne
salt
Equipment: 1 terrine; 1 skimmer; 1 small saucepan;
1 fine sieve; 1 small, shallow dish

■ The day before, preheat oven to 100°C, cut the lobe of foie gras in two and devein. Add salt, pepper and sugar. Place the foie gras in a covered terrine, put this in a bain-marie and bake for 1 hr.

■ With the skimmer, remove the excess grease and allow to cool for 1 hr at room temperature. Refrigerate for 12 hrs.

■ To make the tea jelly, soak the gelatine in cold water. Once softened, drain and fold into the pre-warmed Tarry Souchong tea jelly; strain, add the champagne, salt and allow to cool. Then pour into a small shallow dish and allow to set for 4-6 hrs in the refrigerator.

■ The next day, serve the terrine in slices, with cubes of jelly.

■ *Smoked tea is made with large, already oxidized leaves ("souchong"), roasted then placed on a fresh pine fire. This pine or spruce scent characterises high-quality smoked teas. The intensity of smoking is variable: Tarry Souchong represents the most sustained. Here it is used to perfume a sweet jelly, sold in pots (in department stores and specialist tea shops). It is used as a classic jam or in the making of sauces. There are numerous flavours available.*

Cod steak

Serves 4
Preparation time: 35-40 mins
Cooking time: 5 mins for the spinach;
7-10 mins for the cod
4 cod steaks, between 80-100 g each
3½ tsp Alexandra-David-Néel tea leaves powdered in a blender (box opposite)
1 kg fresh spinach on the stalk
1 knob of butter
olive oil
salt, pepper
Equipment: a blender; cling film; 1 steamer; 1 large saucepan

32

■ Cut the cod steaks in 2 across their thickness, but without dividing them completely. Season with salt and pepper, and sprinkle generously with tea powder. Then re-close. Wrap each piece in cling film, in well-sealed parcels. Place them in the steamer and cook for 7-10 mins, according to the thickness and your preference. Once cooked, allow to rest for 1 min in the cling film, before unwrapping (to allow the tea to continue flavouring the flesh).

■ Meanwhile, cook the spinach (previously de-stalked and washed) with the butter, in the large saucepan. Salt lightly after cooking.
■ Prepare 4 plates. Decorate each plate with a parcel of fish on a bed of spinach and a dash of olive oil.

■ *Alexandra-David-Néel tea (named after the writer, philosopher and explorer, the first Westerner to enter the holy city of Lhasa, Tibet) is a black tea enhanced with a wide range of spices (including pepper, ginger, and cardamom) and with a fresh, floral note.*
If unavailable, choose a tea with mixed spices or cinnamon, cloves, etc.

Chandernagor veal medallions

Serves 4

Preparation time: 1 hr

Cooking time: 50 mins in total

1 x 1.5 kg boneless rack of 4 prime veal chops,

pared, and divided into 4 thick slices

4 baby custard marrows

5 large potatoes

20 cl veal juices (or veal stock)

5 tsp Chandernagor tea leaves

(box opposite)

5 cl sunflower oil

20 g butter

5 cl olive oil

salt, pepper

Equipment: 3 saucepans; 1 whisk; 1 fine sieve;

1 frying pan

■ Cook the baby marrows in boiling, salted water, taking care that they remain crunchy. Boil the potatoes without peeling them. Let them cool then peel and cube. Keep warm.

■ Reduce the veal juices. Briefly infuse the tea in the juices (around 45 secs) whisking all the while. Strain and reduce again to a coating consistency. Check the seasoning and then keep warm.

■ Sear the four pieces of veal in the frying pan with the sunflower oil and 5 g of butter, turning occasionally.

■ Put the potatoes in a saucepan with the rest of the butter and the olive oil and mash with a fork. Add salt and pepper.

■ Garnish each plate with a little mashed potato, place a slice of veal on top, add a baby marrow and drizzle on a ribbon of tea sauce.

■ *Chandernagor, a blend of black tea and spices – cloves, cinnamon, ginger, cardamom and pepper –, recalls the name of one of the five French trading posts in India. Warm to the palate, it easily lifts numerous recipes with no need to add other condiments or seasonings. It can be replaced by other flavoured black teas, as long as they are well-spiced.*

34

Scallops with vegetables and Tarry Souchong tea oil

Serves 4

Preparation time: 50 mins

Infusion: 6 hrs

Cooking time: 3 mins for the mooli (Chinese radish);

2 mins for the carrots; 1 min for the courgettes;

5 mins for the scallops

16 fine, shelled scallops

3 dl sunflower oil

4 tsp Tarry Souchong tea leaves

(boxes opposite and page 30)

500 g mooli (Chinese radish)

500 g carrots

500 g courgettes

1 knob of butter

salt, pepper

Equipment: 3 saucepans (1 large, 2 medium);

1 blender; 1 fine sieve; 1 steamer

■ The day before, warm the oil, stir in the tea, add salt and pepper, blend and keep warm to infuse for at least 6 hrs.

■ The next day, stir the tea oil again and then strain it and keep warm.

■ Chop the vegetables into julienne strips and blanch them. Make sure they stay crunchy.

■ At the last moment, steam the previously cleaned scallops. Sauté the vegetables in the butter, over a gentle heat.

■ Place a mound of vegetables on each plate. Arrange the scallops around the vegetables and drizzle with the Tarry Souchong tea oil.

■ *According to an XVIIth century Chinese legend, smoked tea was created in a factory where an Imperial Army troop, travelling through the region, had decided to stay. The workshops were then full of freshly harvested tea shoots that needed processing without delay. So the artisans, to save time, lit pine fires in order to speed up the drying of the leaves. These took up the smell of the wood fumes: smoked tea had just been invented.*

Duck kebabs with Ruschka tea

Serves 4

Preparation time: 30 mins

Marinating time: 6 hrs

Cooking time: 10 mins

16 slices duck breast fillet

6 tbs olive oil

8 fresh figs

1 x 200 g can grapes in syrup

3 tbs honey

salt, pepper

For the marinade:

½ glass cane syrup

1 tbs Ruschka tea leaves

(box opposite)

½ glass lemon juice

½ glass orange juice

½ glass soy sauce

1 tsp orange zest

1 tsp lemon zest

salt, pepper

Equipment: *1 citrus press; 1 saucepan; 1 fine sieve;*

4 skewers; 1 non-stick frying pan; 1 strainer

▓ For the marinade, heat the cane syrup, add the Ruschka tea, the lemon and orange juice, the soy sauce, and season to taste. When this process is complete, filter everything and then add the orange and lemon zests.

▓ Thread the duck breast slices onto the skewers (4 slices per kebab) and leave to marinate for 6 hrs.

▓ Take the kebabs out of the marinade and cook them in the frying pan in hot oil, 2 mins on each side. Remove the kebabs and keep warm. Put the figs, cut in 2, the drained grapes and the honey into the frying pan, and glaze for 5 mins. Remove the fruit and keep warm.

▓ Deglaze the frying pan with the marinade; cook down until you have a coating sauce. Serve the kebabs with the sauce, accompanied by the figs and grapes, with a green salad and fines herbes on the side.

38

▓ *Ruschka is a flavoured black tea with fruit and citrus essences and enhanced with silver tips (young tea buds). It is at once generous, lively, full and long in the mouth. Other citrus tea blends are suitable for this recipe in place of Ruschka.*

Matcha salt

For 100 g of Matcha salt
Preparation time: 10 mins
75 g of table salt
12½ tsp of powdered Matcha green tea
(boxes opposite and page 20)
Equipment: 1 mixing bowl; 1 blender;
1 airtight storage container

40

■ Combine the salt and tea then blend lightly. Place immediately in an airtight, opaque container, in order to preserve the beautiful jade-green colour of the tea.

■ You can sprinkle Matcha salt onto breakfast boiled eggs, crunchy vegetables, fish or white meats at lunchtime and onto rice, salad, soups, etc. for dinner.

■ *This preparation can be made in advance if the salt used is high-quality (white, iodised and fluorinated and very fine, so that the tea is thoroughly blended), and will keep for 1 month if stored away from light, heat and humidity. Nevertheless, it is advisable, since this is a high quality and high cost tea, to make only small quantities at a time.*

Salmon tartare with Matcha tea

42

Serves 4
Preparation time: 20 mins
600 g salmon fillet
2 tbs snipped chives
1 lemon
6 tbs olive oil
1 tsp powdered Matcha green tea
(box page 20)
salt, pepper
Equipment: 1 salad bowl; 1 citrus press;
1 blender; 1 whisk

▢ Remove any bones from the salmon fillet, cut into small cubes about 5 mm each side. Place this salmon tartare in the salad bowl; add a spoonful of chives, the juice of the lemon and a spoonful of olive oil; season and mix. Set aside.

▢ Then prepare the Matcha oil: blend the remainder of the oil with the rest of the chives; add the Matcha tea powder, blend everything together, whisking well; season.

▢ Serve the tartare on plates, accompanied by a green salad and with the Matcha oil on the side: everyone can help themselves.

Sea bream en croûte with carrot tagliatelle

44

Serves 4
Preparation time: 50 mins
Cooking time: 30 s for the tagliatelle;
6-7 mins for the sea bream
4 skinned fillets of sea bream
800 g carrots
100 g fine breadcrumbs
(home made, if possible from leftover dry bread)
2½ tsp powdered Matcha green tea
(box page 20)
20 cl olive oil
1 knob of butter
salt, pepper
Equipment: 1 vegetable peeler; 1 ovenproof dish;
1 large saucepan

■ Wash and peel the carrots. Cut in half lengthwise. Using the vegetable peeler, cut the carrots into ribbons to make the "tagliatelle". Rinse them and keep chilled.

■ Mix the breadcrumbs and Matcha tea. Add a pinch of salt and some pepper, then blend in 10 cl of olive oil until you have a smooth, bright green mixture.

■ Cook the sea bream fillets in the oven with a dash of olive oil. Halfway through cooking, put an even layer of the green breadcrumbs over each fillet and finish cooking under the grill.

■ Drop the carrot tagliatelle into a saucepan of boiling water, and take them out again before it comes back to the boil. Add butter.

■ Serve the sea bream, surrounded by tagliatelle and drizzle the remaining olive oil over it all.

Green tea parcels

Serves 4
Preparation time: 30 mins
Cooking time: 5 mins
4 sheets brick pastry
(like filo, but finer and more crepe-like in texture)
200 g crab meat
1 chopped onion
1 bunch snipped chives
20 g butter
1 tsp powdered Matcha green tea (box page 20)
salt, pepper
Equipment: 1 fine sieve; 1 pastry brush;
1 non-stick frying pan

■ Mix the crab meat, onion, chives and season lightly with salt and pepper.

■ Soften the butter (cut into cubes, heat for a few seconds in the microwave, mash with a fork). To avoid lumps, sift in the Matcha. Brush the brick pastry leaves with the Matcha butter.

■ Spread the crab meat in the centre of each leaf, fold up the sides to make a triangle or a square. Cook for 5 mins in the frying pan, turning the parcels halfway through cooking.

■ Accompanied by salad, the parcels – which are served piping hot – can be a main course or enjoyed as an appetizer.

■ *Matcha butter, such as the one made here, can also be used to butter toast, boiled egg "soldiers", or even canapés with salmon, prawns etc.*

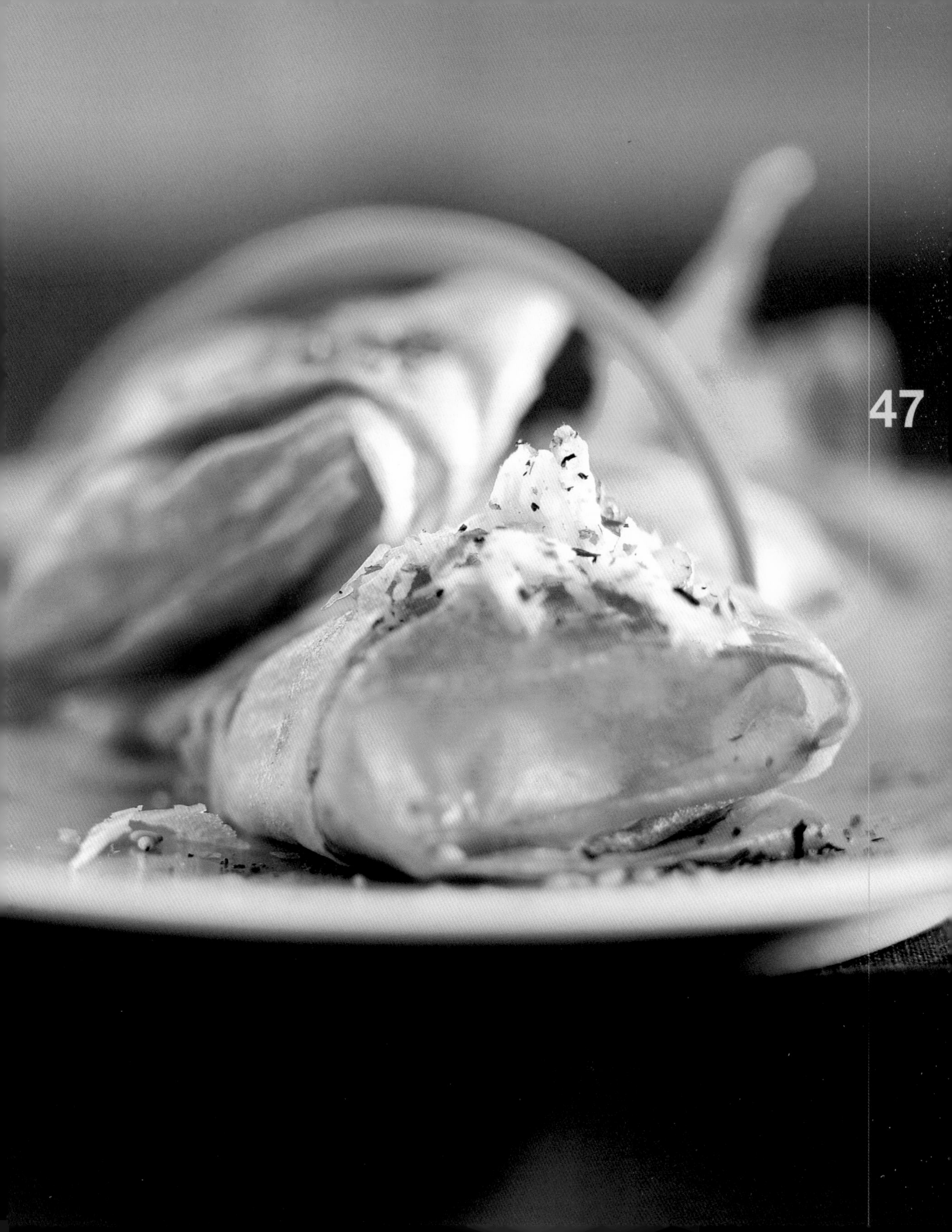

Pigeon with Thé sur le Nil

Serves 6
Preparation time: 45 mins
Cooking time: 30-35 mins
6 plucked and drawn pigeons
1 large onion, thinly sliced
1 carrot, thinly sliced
6 tbs olive oil
1 glass orange juice
1 glass white wine
1 sprig of thyme
1 clove of garlic
1 chicken stock cube
1 stick cinnamon
2 star anise
2 tbs Thé sur le Nil leaves
(box opposite)
400 g medium couscous
75 g pine nuts
50 g sultanas
1 tbs chopped flat leaf parsley
1 tbs chopped coriander
salt, pepper
Equipment: 1 casserole dish; 1 fine strainer;
1 skimmer; 1 large non-stick frying pan

■ Preheat the oven to 180°C. Put the pigeons in the casserole dish with their giblets, onion, carrot and 2 spoonfuls of olive oil. Season and bake. After 10 mins, add the orange juice, white wine, thyme, peeled garlic, stock cube, cinnamon and star anise, cover and cook for 15-20 mins, basting frequently.

■ After cooking, take the pigeons out of the oven and keep warm. Add 1 tbs of tea leaves to the cooking juices and allow to steep for 5 mins, strain, skim off the excess grease and season the gravy to taste. Keep warm.

■ Brown the couscous in the frying pan in the remaining olive oil with the pine nuts and sultanas; pour in 75 cl of salted water, cover and cook for 2 mins over a gentle heat; add the remaining tea leaves. Leave the couscous to swell off the heat, separate the grains well, and then add parsley and coriander.

■ Serve the pigeons drizzled with gravy and accompanied by couscous.

■ Thé sur le Nil is made up of fine Sencha green teas which are mixed with citrus fruits with citronella and spice notes. Lively, fresh, particularly fruity, it goes well with fish and exotic dishes. It can be replaced by a citrus green tea.

48

Tagliatelle and "sesame green tea"

Serves 4
Preparation time: 15 mins
Cooking time: about 10 mins total
500 g fresh tagliatelle
1 punnet of cherry tomatoes
10 cl olive oil
"sesame green tea" (box page 22)
1 bunch of chives or basil, chopped
salt, pepper
Equipment: 1 large saucepan; 1 frying pan;
1 colander

■ Cook the tagliatelle in boiling water (8 mins if they are homemade and if you like them al dente). Meanwhile, fry the cherry tomatoes in the olive oil.

■ Drain the pasta. Fold in the basil or chives, season to taste with salt, pepper, "sesame green tea" and a dash of olive oil.

■ Divide the tagliatelle and tomatoes between 4 plates.

■ *This recipe can be made with vegetable tagliatelle – mooli, courgettes, carrots (see page 44) – following the same process.*

50

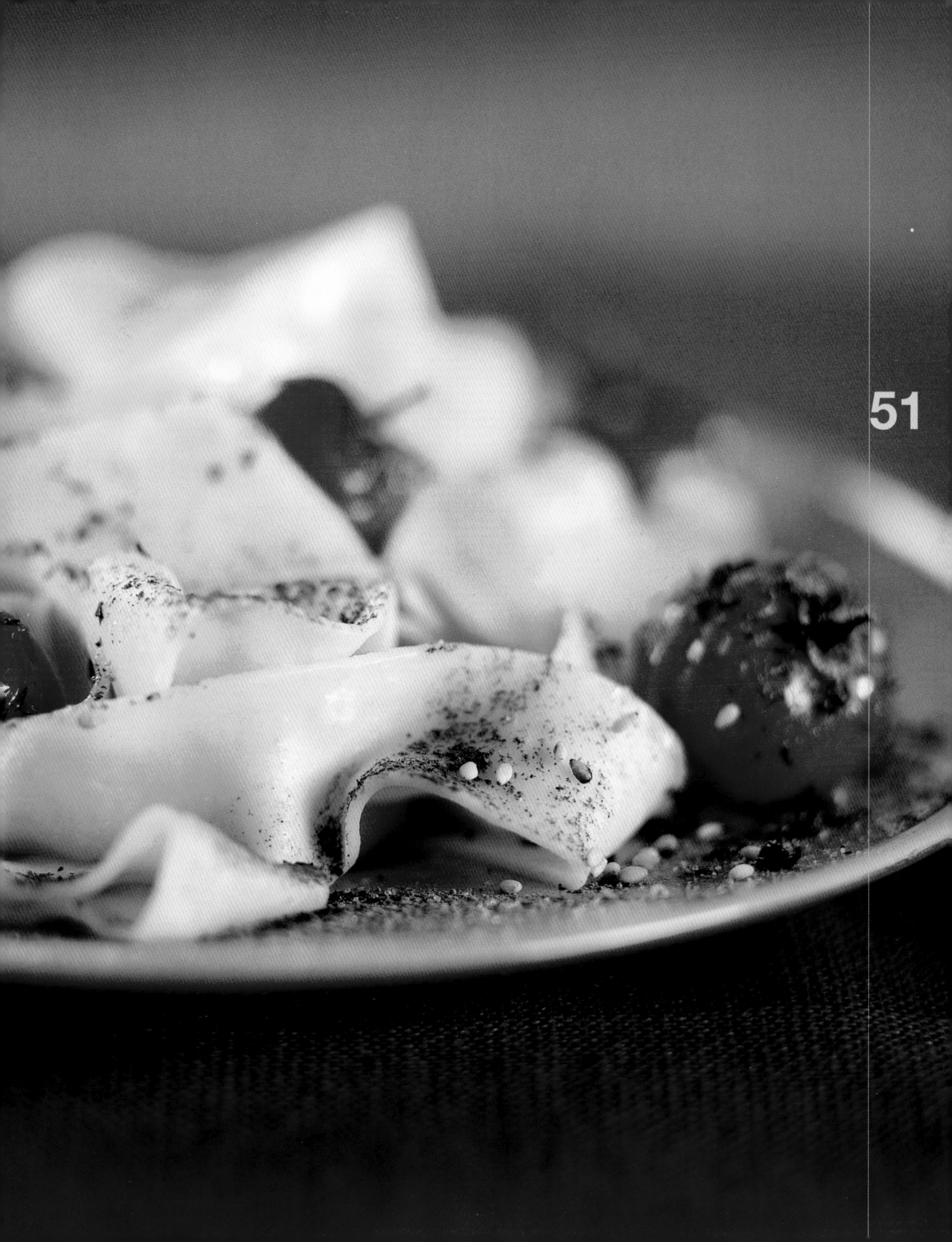

Baked eggs

Serves 4

Preparation time: 35 mins

Cooking time: 7 mins

2½ tsp La Route du Temps tea leaves

(box opposite)

1 knob of butter

4 eggs

30 cl whipping cream

salt, pepper

Equipment: 1 blender; 1 small saucepan;

1 whisk; 1 fine strainer; 4 ramekins

■ Put the tea leaves in the blender bowl and reduce to a powder.

■ Butter the 4 ramekins and break 1 egg into each of them. It is best to use small ramekins, the size of a cup, so that the egg yolk appears centred.

■ Reduce the cream by a third in the small saucepan on a gentle heat. Mix the tea powder and the cream, whisking well. Strain. Season with salt and pepper.

Pour this mixture of cream and tea onto the eggs and cook for 7 mins on a gentle heat (120°C) or in a bain-marie. Serve immediately. Salmon roe could be sprinkled on top.

■ If you are preparing this the previous day, you can steep the tea powder in the cold cream; then mix the tea and cream in a ramekin, cover with cling film and place in the refrigerator. The next day, mix well before use.

■ *La Route du Temps tea combines the fresh taste of green teas from the mountainous plantations in the north of Thailand and the spice notes of pieces of ginger. The whole is enhanced with the light taste of honey.*

A pure ginger green tea, a jasmine tea or one with gentle spices will make up an appealing alternative and allow subtle variations.

52

Cream of asparagus soup

Serves 4

Preparation time: 50 mins

Cooking time: 35 mins

2 bunches white asparagus

1 l chicken stock

1 egg yolk

4 tbs double cream

1½ tsp powdered Matcha green tea

(box page 20)

100 g cleaned chanterelle mushrooms

1 knob of butter

4 small pieces smoked haddock

Equipment: 1 large saucepan; 1 blender; 1 whisk;

1 fine strainer; 1 non-stick frying pan; 4 bowls

■ Wash and peel the asparagus, drop into chicken stock and cook until they are very tender. Then blend the stock and asparagus. Add the egg yolk and cream, whisk to thicken and fold in the Matcha tea, whisking continually. Strain and keep warm.

■ Fry the chanterelles very quickly in a little butter. Divide the soup between the 4 bowls, place the chanterelles in a circle around the edge. Then fry the pieces of smoked haddock for a few seconds and place them, warm, in the centre of the bowls.

■ *Many teas blend harmoniously with soups. The choice will depend on the ingredients used in the soup. For example, we recommend a spicy black tea (like Chandernagor – box page 34) for a pumpkin soup, a Tarry Souchong (boxes pages 30 and 36) for a carrot consommé, or a Matcha for a spinach cream soup.*

Freshly ground tea

Preparation time: 5 mins

6 tbs Éros tea (box opposite)

10 g black peppercorns

Equipment: 1 pepper mill, preferably equipped with a grind regulating mechanism

■ Mix the pepper and tea leaves then pour into the mill. Allow 25% pepper to 75% tea. Regulate the grind, if your mill has the necessary device.

■ Use this blend as a cooking or table condiment (available to all diners) to season meats and bring out their other flavours.

■ Take care always to turn the mill mechanism in the same direction, not going backwards and forwards, in order not to use it up too soon and to avoid reducing the leaves to an inconsistent powder.

■ This preparation should only be made in small quantities to keep it fresh.

■ *With black teas, use black pepper. Harvested at half maturity, this is a little more piquant and aromatic than white pepper. Éros tea, suggested here, is a black tea flavoured with hibiscus flowers and dotted with mallow flowers. All the Chinese black tea blends with floral aromas are perfect for meat, poultry or fried foie gras.*

■ *With green teas, use white pepper. Harvested at full maturity, this pepper has a hot taste and a spicy perfume, and has the advantage of not discolouring delicate sauces with black dots. Thé sur le Nil (box page 48), among others, is well-suited to this type of blend and perfectly seasons fish, shellfish and salad dressings.*

■ *Lastly, you can of course use the mill without pepper, grinding just the tea leaves. In this case choose green teas with large tender leaves.*

Tofu and mixed vegetables with Bouddha Bleu tea

Serves 4

Preparation and cooking time: 20 mins total

300 g firm tofu (Asian grocery)

40 g shiitake mushrooms (Asian grocers)

4 cherry tomatoes

4 baby leeks

4 baby courgettes

4 baby fennel bulbs

4 baby marrows

4 stems green asparagus

4 carrot tops

50 g peas

100 g mange tout

100 g French beans

8 Chinese cabbage leaves

8 tbs soy sauce

1 tbs Bouddha Bleu tea leaves

(box opposite)

2 tbs sesame oil

1 tsp cornflower petals (herbalist)

4 sprigs chervil

salt, pepper

Equipment: 2 saucepans (1 large and 1 small);

1 fine strainer; 1 non-stick frying pan; 1 salad bowl

58

■ Cook all the vegetables (except the tomatoes and mushrooms) in boiling water, making sure that they stay crunchy. Set aside.

■ For the sauce, heat the soy sauce, add the tea leaves, allow to steep for 2 mins and then strain. Keep warm.

■ Cut the tofu into 1.5 cm thick cubes and sauté them in very hot sesame oil. When the tofu is golden on both sides, add the mushrooms and all the pre-cooked vegetables and sauté for 2-3 mins; season. Remove from the heat and add the cherry tomatoes.

■ Serve the tofu and vegetables piping hot, drizzled with the sauce. Sprinkle on the cornflower petals (for visual appeal) and a few chervil leaves.

■ *Bouddha Bleu is made up of green tea enhanced with cornflower leaves and ripe fruits.*
Blends with dominant berry or citrus aromas add an original note to vegetables and tofu.

Red mullet with mango chutney and Festin d'Or tea

Serves 4
Preparation time: 30 mins
Cooking time: 30 mins total
Refrigeration: 2 hrs
4 red mullets about 400 g scaled and filleted
2 tbs olive oil
400 g spinach leaves, washed well
400 g julienne of vegetables
(finely chopped carrots, celery, turnips, courgettes)
salt, pepper
For the dressing:
6 tbs sesame oil
2 tbs red rice vinegar (Asian grocery)
1 tbs Festin d'Or tea leaves (box opposite)
salt, pepper
For the sauce:
2 mangoes
1 jar (200 g) mango chutney (Indian grocery)
2 tbs currants
1 tbs Festin d'Or tea leaves
salt, pepper
Equipment: 1 blender; 1 medium saucepan;
1 non-stick frying pan; 1 salad bowl; cling film

■ For the dressing, blend the oil, vinegar and the tea leaves, season and set aside.

■ For the sauce, peel the mangoes and cut them into 1 cm cubes; put them to cook on a gentle heat with the chutney and currants, simmer gently for about 20 mins. Add the tea leaves, season, cover with cling film and leave aside in the refrigerator for 2 hrs.

■ Season the mullet fillets and fry them in very hot olive oil for 5 mins on the skin side and then 5 mins on the flesh side.

■ In a large salad bowl, combine the julienne of raw vegetables and spinach leaves, season with the Festin d'Or dressing. Place the fillets onto this salad, serve the mango sauce separately.

■ *Festin d'Or marries green tea and bunches of marigold and Moroccan mint. The rich perfume of fresh mint and the powerful floral fragrances evoke the Orient. In a drink, this tea tastes as good hot as cold.*
You can replace it with green floral or mint teas.

Sole salad with Pharaon tea

Serves 4

Preparation time: 20 mins

Cooking time: 15 mins

2 skinless sole fillets about 400 g each

1 tbs Pharaon tea leaves

(box opposite)

2 tbs olive oil

1 mango

salt, pepper

For the dressing:

3 tbs lemon juice

3 tbs orange juice

1 tbs Pharaon tea leaves

6 tbs olive oil

1 tbs chopped chervil

salt, pepper

Equipment: 1 ovenproof dish; 1 citrus press;

1 saucepan; 1 whisk; 1 fine strainer

■ Preheat the oven to 220°C. Garnish each sole fillet with a little Pharaon tea. Season the fillets after garnishing, then roll them up, place in an oiled ovenproof dish, bake for around 7 mins and then allow to cool to room temperature.

■ For the dressing, pour the lemon and orange juices into a saucepan and bring to the boil; then add the Pharaon tea and beat in the olive oil with a whisk. Strain the dressing, add the chopped chervil. Season.

■ Peel the mango, cut it into slivers.

■ Serve the fillets coated in dressing, garnish everything with mango rosettes, and serve with a bunch of green salad.

■ *Pharaon tea is an Indian green tea scented with fruits of the Nile delta. As a substitute, choose other green teas with essence of citrus, ripe or exotic fruits.*

62

Monkfish slices with grapefruit sauce with Ylang Ylang tea

64

Serves 4
Preparation time: 20 mins
Cooking time: 10 mins
600 g headless, boneless monkfish fillet
2 grapefruits
200 g butter
1 tbs cornflour
1 tbs Ylang Ylang tea leaves
(box opposite)
2 tbs olive oil
salt, pepper
Equipment: 1 citrus press; 1 saucepan; 1 whisk;
1 fine strainer; 1 frying pan

■ Cut the monkfish into medallions 1 cm in thickness. Peel 1 grapefruit thoroughly and separate into quarters (removing the membrane).

■ Squeeze the second grapefruit, boil the juice obtained, add the butter in small quantities and whisk; blend in the cornflour mixed with ½ glass of water to thicken the sauce; add the Ylang Ylang tea leaves and remove from the heat. Allow to steep for 2 mins, strain, add salt and pepper. Keep warm.

■ Cook the monkfish slices in the frying pan in very hot olive oil, 2 mins on each side.

■ Serve the monkfish garnished with quarters of grapefruit and coated in sauce, accompanied by rice and vegetables.

■ *Under the influence of French perfumiers, the Ylang Ylang tree has become widespread around the Indian Ocean (especially in the Comoros and Madagascar). Today it is cultivated in tropical Asia and the north of Australia as an ornamental tree and above all for its sweet-smelling green or yellow flowers which provide a highly sought-after essential oil. On a base of black tea, the ripe and freshly-harvested flowers produce a very floral, soft and heady mix.*

Braised calf's livers with Marco Polo tea

Serves 4
Preparation time: 1 hr
Cooking time: 35 mins for the sauce
8 mins for the livers;
6-8 mins for the pasta
4 slices of calf's liver
100 g of spiced bread crumbs (grate them yourself)
1 spring onion, chopped
30 g flour
10 cl olive oil
15 cl white vinegar
50 g sugar
20 cl veal stock
5 tsp Marco Polo tea leaves
(box opposite)
1 knob of butter
320 g fresh pasta (preferably tagliatelle)
salt
Equipment: 3 saucepans (1 large and 2 small);
1 fine strainer; 1 whisk; 1 non-stick frying pan

■ Mix the spiced bread crumbs with the onion. Coat each slice of liver in the flour, in the olive oil then in the breadcrumbs and set aside (it is best to do this at the last moment).

■ In a saucepan, reduce the vinegar, sugar and a little salt to a very thick consistency, ensuring it is not allowed to caramelise. At the same time, heat the veal stock, steep the tea in it (for about 1 min) and strain. Add this mixture to the sweet sauce, whisking well and reduce until the preparation has a shiny, coating consistency

■ Cook the pasta and fry the calf's livers in a little butter and salt them lightly. Divide between the plates. Serve the sauce separately, in a sauceboat, to preserve the crunchiness of the breadcrumbs.

■ *Marco Polo is a floral, fruity black tea, from China and Tibet. Highly perfumed, combining many fruity flavours, it has a very strong fragrance before infusion and a subtle taste once in the cup, the whole having a really lasting flavour. Its aromas suggest vanilla, berries or exotic fruits, offering a perfect balance of strength and mellowness. This recipe may also be the opportunity to try a spiced or boldly fruity black tea.*

Filet mignon with Bourbon tea

Serves 6
Preparation and cooking time: 35 mins in total
2 filets mignon of pork about 600 g each
2 tbs olive oil
4 chopped shallots
4 tbs clear honey
1 tsp powdered cinnamon
1 glass white wine
1 vanilla pod
1 glass orange juice
2 tbs Bourbon tea leaves
(box opposite)
salt, pepper
Equipment: 1 non-stick frying pan; 1 lid; 1 citrus press;
1 coffee grinder; 1 pastry brush

■ Devein each filet mignon and season. Brown the filets in the frying pan, in the olive oil, then add the shallots, cover and cook gently.

■ After 5 mins, add the honey, cinnamon, white wine, vanilla pod cut in two, orange juice and the tea (previously powdered in the coffee grinder); leave to simmer for a further 10 mins, stirring frequently.

■ Slice the filets diagonally and brush with the sauce. Serve with mashed potatoes or sautéed vegetables.

■ *Bourbon tea is a member of the red "tea" family, coming not from the tea plant Camellia Sinensis but from a bush known as Borbonia Pinifolia which grows in South Africa. This type of naturally theine-free tea is very rich in vitamin C, mineral salts and protein. It can be drunk iced or hot, morning or evening, with or without milk, natural or with added flavours.*

The red tea known as "Bourbon" is flavoured with bourbon vanilla. It may be replaced by a mild whole-leaf tea, flavoured with natural vanilla.

■ *Note that there are all sorts of red teas, for example Métis (box page 16) with citrus flavours, spices, fruits and flowers; or, again, Nil Rouge tea (see page 84).*

Perfumed Chantilly cream

Serves 4
Preparation time: 10 mins
Cold infusion: 1 – 8 hrs
10 tsp tea leaves
(select variety according to taste)
500 ml whipping cream
75 g icing sugar
Equipment: 1 salad bowl to infuse the tea;
1 fine strainer; 1 electric or hand whisk;
1 container for assembling the Chantilly cream

70

■ Make a cold infusion of the tea in the whipping cream. According to the tea chosen, the infusion time will vary: 1 hr for smoked teas, 4 hrs for black teas, 8 hrs for red teas or green teas.

■ Once the infusion is finished, strain the tea cream. Add the icing sugar and beat with the electric or hand whisk as for a classic whipped cream.

■ Garnish this Chantilly cream, if desired, with fresh fruit (raspberries, strawberries, blackberries) or serve as an accompaniment to fruit cake, pound cake, dry biscuits, etc.

■ *If you don't have enough time to infuse the tea, beat the whipping cream and sugar together without previous infusion. Then simply sprinkle on Poudre de jade tea (made from Matcha Uji – box page 20). This tea adds a new twist to all sweet dishes, from pastries to pancakes, including ice cream, cream, desserts, but also buttered toast, yoghurt, fruit salad, cold or warm milk.*

Crème brûlée with Marco Polo tea

Serves 4-5

Preparation time: 15 mins

Refrigeration: 24 hrs

Cooking time: 1 hr

1 dl milk

7½ tsp Marco Polo tea leaves

(box page 66)

8 egg yolks

130 g caster sugar

500 ml single cream

40 g soft brown sugar

Equipment: 2 saucepans; 1 whisk; 1 fine strainer;

4-5 ramekins

■ The day before, heat the milk in a saucepan, and add the tea, allowing it to infuse for 3 minutes. Meanwhile, whisk the egg yolks and sugar until they turn white.

■ Strain the milk and tea infusion, then decant this infusion into another saucepan with the single cream. Heat, then pour onto the egg yolks and sugar, whisking well. Pass this mixture through a fine strainer and allow to rest in the refrigerator for 24 hrs.

■ The next day, preheat the oven to 90°C. Divide the mixture between the ramekins and bake for 1 hr. When the preparation is the consistency of a crème caramel, take the ramekins out of the oven, allow to cool and keep in the refrigerator.

■ To serve, take the crèmes out of refrigerator, sprinkle with soft brown sugar and caramelise under the grill. You can garnish them with raspberries or young mint leaves. Enjoy immediately.

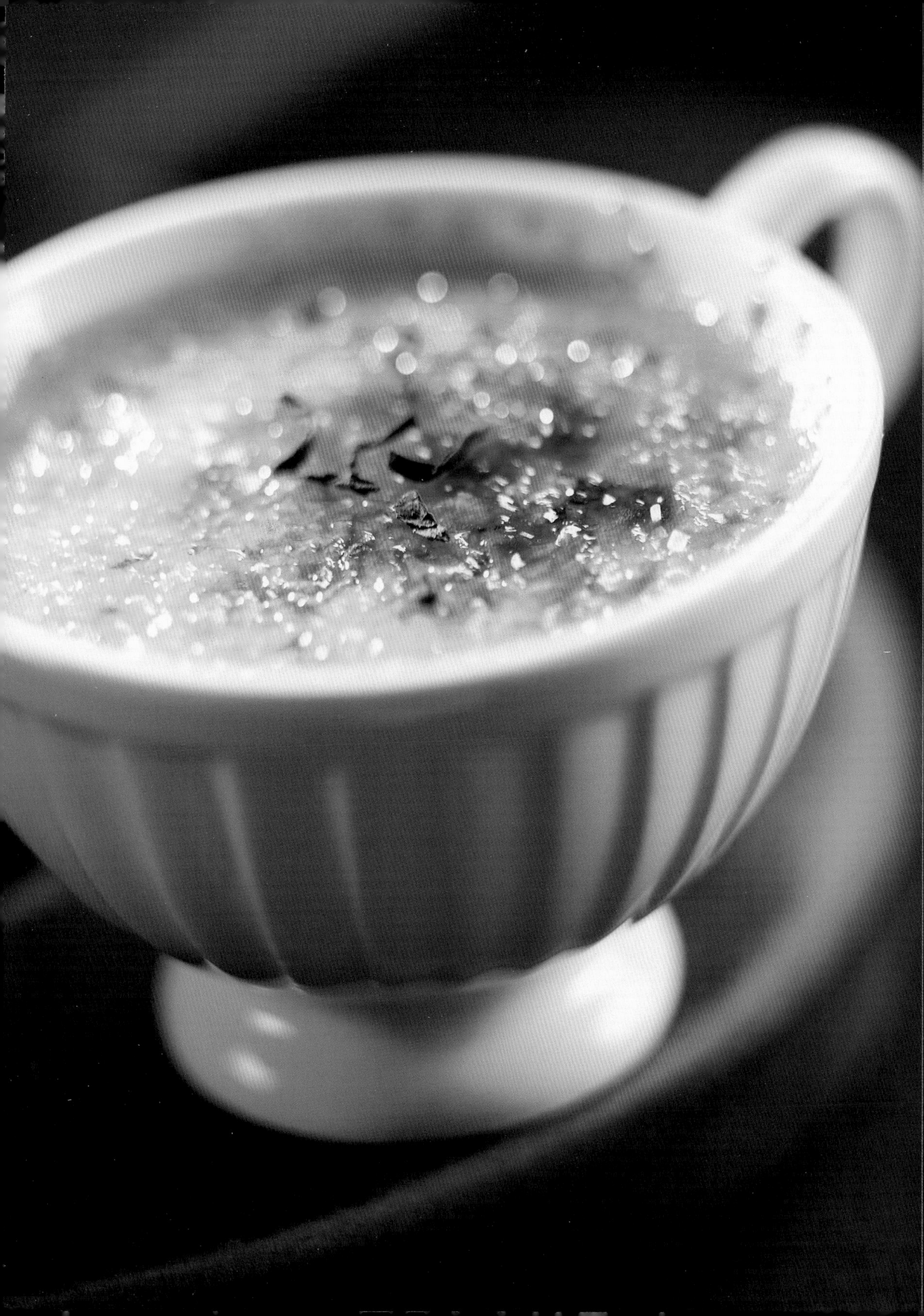

Financier cakes with Matcha tea

74

Serves 4-6
Preparation time: 15-20 mins
Refrigeration: 24 hrs
Cooking time: 15-20 mins
50 g ground almonds
150 g caster sugar
4 egg whites
50 g flour
2½ tsp powdered Matcha green tea
(box page 20)
140 g butter
Equipment: 1 electric whisk; 1 sieve; 1 saucepan;
1 fine strainer; 1 airtight container;
1 piping bag and nozzle; financier tins

■ The day before, whisk together the ground almonds, sugar and 1/3 of the egg whites, to a smooth paste (the initially quite dense mixture is gradually thinned by the egg whites).

■ Sift the flour and tea together. Pour over the first mixture, being careful not to allow lumps to form. Whisk until smooth.

■ Heat the butter gently in the saucepan until it forms a brown butter (a hazelnut smell is characteristic). Strain this butter and blend it into the previous preparation until smooth.

■ Put the mixture into an airtight container and allow to rest in the refrigerator for 24 hrs.

■ The next day, preheat the oven to 165°C. Using the piping bag and nozzle, 2/3 fill the financier tins and bake for 15 mins. Take out of the oven, and, if using metal tins remove from tins immediately or if using Exopan (flexible moulds) allow to cool first. Enjoy warm or cool.

Fresh fruit in Festin d'Or syrup

Serves 6

Preparation time: 15-20 mins

1 mango

1 papaya

2 kiwi fruit

2 bananas

1 small pineapple

2 passion fruit

1 small bunch mint

For the syrup:

5 tsp Festin d'Or tea leaves (box page 60)

10 g pectin

100 g sugar

Equipment: *1 saucepan ; 1 cotton tea strainer*

■ Peel and deseed the fruit, (put the passion fruit seeds to one side), slice and set aside.

■ To make the syrup, steep the tea in 25 cl hot water (for around 3 mins), strain the infusion pressing lightly on the tea leaves collected in the cotton strainer; then boil this infusion. Mix the pectin and sugar then pour it into the infusion over the heat. Boil once, remove from the heat, and allow to cool. Keep cool.

■ Arrange the fruit in rosettes on the plates: before serving, pour a little cold syrup onto each fruit arrangement, then garnish with the passion fruit seeds and chopped mint.

Esprit de Noël dried fruit salad and ice cream

78

Serves 4

Preparation time: 10 mins for the ice cream;

15 mins for the fruit salad

Refrigeration: 24 hrs

For the ice cream:

25 cl milk

5 tsp Esprit de Noël tea

(box opposite)

160 g caster sugar

2 egg yolks

60 g single cream.

For the fruit salad:

50 g sultanas

50 g dried apricots

50 g dried figs

20 g crushed, roasted hazelnuts

20 g crushed pistachios

25 g butter

50 g Esprit de Noël tea jelly (box page 30)

20 g Esprit de Noël tea infusion (box opposite)

Equipment: 2 saucepans; 1 whisk; 1 fine strainer;

1 ice cream maker;

■ For the ice cream: boil the milk and steep the tea for about 2 to 3 mins. Fold 60 g of sugar into the egg yolks, whisking until the mixture turns white. Strain the milk and tea infusion then decant into a saucepan with the rest of the sugar. Boil again, pour onto the egg yolks and sugar and cook over a gentle heat for 5 mins, stirring continually with a wooden spoon. Strain then fold in the single cream. Leave to cool for 24 hrs. The next day, pour into the ice cream maker (at around - 8 °C). Keep cold (- 12 °C).

■ Prepare the fruit salad by roughly chopping the dried apricots and figs. Melt the butter and add the jelly. When the mixture comes to the boil, blend in all the other ingredients, bring back to the boil and deglaze with the tea infusion.

■ Decorate the plates with warm fruit salad and ice cream balls.

■ *Esprit de Noël tea is a mildly spicy black tea, with orange peel and bourbon vanilla pieces. If unavailable, choose a tea with cloves, cinnamon, ginger, etc.*

Chocolate mousse with Roi des Earl Grey tea

Serves 3-4

Preparation time: 20 mins

3 egg whites

30 g sugar

75 g dark, dessert chocolate

30 g whipping cream.

2½ tsp Roi des Earl Grey tea leaves

(box opposite)

Equipment: 1 salad bowl; 1 saucepan; 1 electric whisk; 1 blender; 3 or 4 ramekins

80

■ Beat the egg whites into peaks and fold them into the sugar until you have a stiff consistency.

■ Melt the chocolate in a bain-marie.

■ Whip the cream with an electric whisk. Reduce the tea to powder in the blender and fold into the whipping cream.

■ Mix the tea cream blend with the melted chocolate and fold in the egg whites.

■ Decorate the little ramekins and garnish to taste with kumquats, candied orange peel, a small bunch of mint, etc.

■ *The smooth yellow bergamot fruit is a citrus fruit whose sweet perfume is highly sought after. It is used in making Earl Grey tea, the recipe for which was brought back from China by the eponymous Earl Grey. It's a traditional blend found in every tea shop. Its quality can be uneven. If possible check the provenance of the bergamot: that from Sicily is most in demand. Don't be deceived by the heaviness of its often volatile fragrance; what counts is what stays in the mouth. The base of tea is an essential element in the success of its composition: avoid the fragments of leaves which give an over-strong taste which lacks subtlety. Choose ideally Yunnan black tea, a Ceylon whole-leaf tea or a Darjeeling, which combine strength and delicacy.*

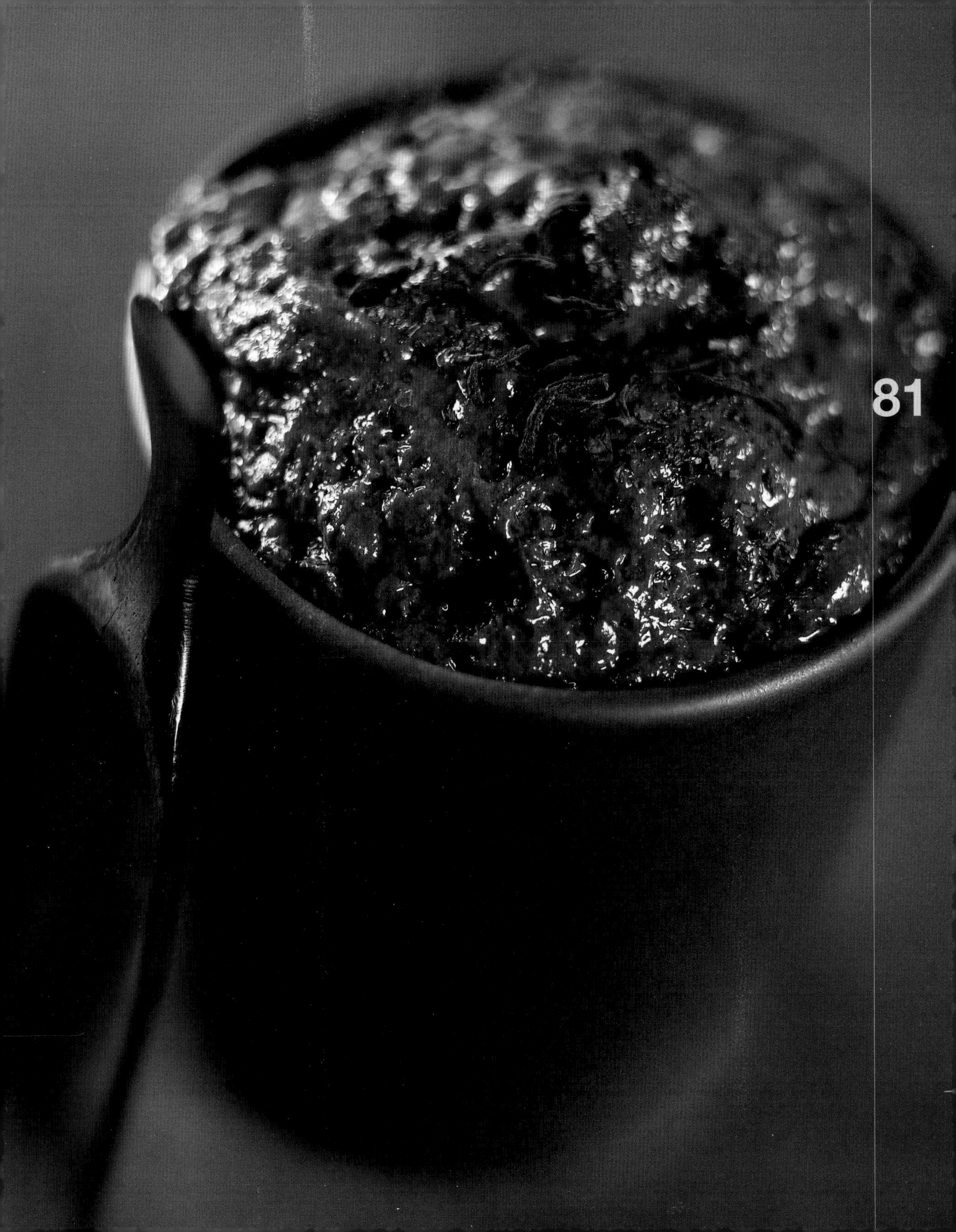

Darjeeling Tart

Serves 4

Preparation time: 45 mins

Chilling time for pastry: 1 hr

Cooking time: 15 mins for the pastry base

Refrigeration of the pastry base: 15-20 mins

For the sweet pastry:

50 g butter + 1 knob of butter for the tart ring

40 g caster sugar

1 egg

100 g flour

For the Darjeeling cream:

10 cl milk

40 cl single cream

20 tsp Margaret's Hope tea leaves

(box opposite)

100 g caster sugar

9 egg yolks

10 g potato starch

2 gelatine leaves

For the meringue:

2 egg whites

100 g caster sugar

Equipment: *1 tart ring for 4 people;*

2 saucepans; 1 fine strainer; 1 whisk;

1 blender; 1 icing bag and nozzle

■ For the sweet pastry: mix the butter and sugar quickly then fold in the egg and flour; make a ball of pastry and keep cool for 1 hr. Preheat the oven to 180°C. Roll out the pastry and use to line the previously greased tart ring. Bake for 10 mins, remove the ring and allow to cool.

■ For the Darjeeling cream: warm the milk and cream and when it's hot pour over the tea leaves. Steep for 5 mins. Strain and bring back to the boil. Whisk the sugar and egg yolks until the preparation turns white, add the potato starch, fold into the tea mixture and allow to cook for about 5 mins. Soften the gelatine and fold into the cream, off the heat. Blend till smooth then add to the tart base. Chill for 15-20 mins.

■ For the meringue, beat the egg whites into peaks. Heat the sugar in a little water to the soft ball stage (113°C-118°C). Whisk this syrup with egg whites. When the meringue is cold, decorate the tart with it, using the piping bag.

■ *Darjeeling is considered the most refined Indian tea. Among the 87 great plantations in the production region, Margaret's Hope produces a very highly regarded autumn harvest tea that has a woody perfume, with a hint of hazelnut.*

Nil Rouge
tea syrup

For 1 l of syrup

Preparation time: 5 mins

Chilling time: 1 hr

1 l mineral water (Volvic, for example)

15 tsp Nil Rouge tea leaves

(box opposite)

20 cl cane syrup

Equipment: 1 teapot or 1 large saucepan;

1 cotton tea strainer

▨ Steep the tea for about 3 to 5 mins in 1 l just-boiling mineral water. Remove the tea leaves.

▨ Add the cane syrup and mix well.

▨ Allow to cool for 1 hr in the refrigerator.

▨ The Nil Rouge is naturally caffeine-free (like all red teas), so can be served anytime, and even to children.

▨ *The tea syrup will keep for a good week in an air-tight container. It can be used to enliven all types of drinks; just adjust the quantity: allow, for example, 1 volume syrup to 9 volumes fruit juice for a non-alcoholic cocktail; for a lightly alcoholic cocktail, allow 1 volume of cane syrup to 5 of sparkling wine.*

▨ *For a quicker, more concentrated extract, pour 1 l syrup into a saucepan, add the tea leaves – 100 g for 1 l – and bring to the boil. Strain. The subtly caramelised combination is ready to dilute to taste.*

▨ *Choose flavoured, floral or fruity teas over too-delicate teas. Or, again, red teas (box page 68) like Nil Rouge tea, a blend of citrus fruits, Oriental spices and marigold flowers, with a flavour at once mild and uplifting.*

Avocado cocktail

For 4 glasses
Preparation time: 10 mins
Refrigeration: 40 mins
1 l mineral water (Volvic, for example)
7½ tsp Thé sur le Nil leaves (box page 48)
½ avocado
salt, pepper
Equipment: 1 teapot or 1 saucepan;
1 cotton tea strainer; 1 blender

▪ Steep the tea for about 2 mins in 1 l just-boiling mineral water. Remove the tea leaves.

▪ Allow to cool for 40 min in the refrigerator.

▪ Peel, de-stone and cut the half-avocado into pieces and put into the blender. Add the infusion and mix everything in the blender bowl.

▪ When a smooth mixture has been achieved, season to taste.

86

▪ *The clear, citronella-accented Thé sur le Nil marries harmoniously here with the softness of the avocado flesh and its walnut and aniseed taste.*

▪ *For a variation, choose another citrus-scented green tea (for the colour), or you may prefer this dish as a sweet cocktail. Use, for example, Thé à l'Opéra – a green tea with berries and spices – and add 10 cl of cane syrup to the avocado-infusion mix. Avoid using fermented teas which have the tendency to blacken the avocado.*

Watermelon juice cocktail

Serves 4
Preparation time: 10 mins
Refrigeration: 1 hr
1 l water (Volvic, for example)
7½ tsp Montagne de Jade tea leaves
(box opposite)
350 g watermelon flesh
10 cl cane syrup
1 tsp coconut powder
***Equipment:** 1 teapot or 1 saucepan;*
1 cotton tea strainer; 1 blender

■ Steep the tea for 2 mins in 1 l just-boiling mineral water. Remove the tea leaves and leave the infusion to cool.

■ Cut the watermelon into pieces and put into the blender. Add the infusion and the cane syrup, and mix everything in the blender bowl. Set aside in the refrigerator for 1 hr.

■ Serve in glasses with grated coconut or coconut powder sprinkled on top.

■ *Montagne de Jade is a Chinese green tea enlivened with exotic fruit. Silky and fragrant, it creates an original marriage between the soft, sweet watermelon and the white, fibrous-fleshed coconut adding a note of fantasy to the cocktail.*

■ *To increase the strength of this recipe, you can also perfume the coconut with tea: soak the coconut powder in tea syrup (see page 84), steep for around 5 hrs then spread out on a baking sheet in a hot oven (180°C). Dry until a crust forms, remove from the oven and grind with a pestle. Allow to cool, and then sprinkle onto the cocktail.*

■ *Numerous fruits and teas lend themselves to this kind of marriage: combine melon, pineapple or mango with green or black, fruity or floral, tea blends.*

Jade Mousse

Serves 4
Preparation time: 5 mins
Refrigeration: 2 hrs
1 l whole milk
8 g powdered Matcha Uji green tea (box page 20)
8 g caster sugar
Equipment: 1 blender

90

■ Pour the milk into the blender, add the tea and sugar.

■ Blend and set aside in the refrigerator for 2 hrs.

■ Before serving, sprinkle a light dusting of Matcha Uji (or Poudre de Jade – box page 70) and serve cold.

■ Enjoy this vitamin-packed – and quick to prepare – drink to start the day. Children who avoid breakfast will appreciate this dense and fragrant mousse with its energy-giving properties. In the same way, suggest this reviving drink after sporting activities.

■ Putting it on the brunch table will bring a refreshing and unexpected note of colour.

■ *The combination of milk and tea is old and widespread. The cloud of fresh milk indicates tea in the English style, sweet and concentrated; it sweetens Cha Thaï – a black, spicy very strong tea from Thailand – among others. The Tibetans themselves most often use a brick of compressed tea onto which they pour boiling water; they then add yak or sheep butter and salt. When the butter melts, the tea is ready to drink...*

■ *We would rather recommend a lassi: bring 20 cl of water to the boil in a saucepan, add 10 g of caster sugar, pour in 5 tsp of Vanille Impériale tea (or another tea, black or green, spiced or vanilla); infuse for about 3 mins then strain. Allow to cool for 1 hr, then put 1 l milk, 3 natural yoghurts and the cool syrup into the blender. Serve immediately.*

Wine with Alexandra-David-Néel tea

Serves 4
Preparation time: 5 mins
75 cl red table wine (an old Gigondas or Chinon,
Burgundy or wine from Herault)
2½ tsp Alexandra-David-Néel tea leaves (box page 32)
10-20 g caster sugar, according to taste
Equipment: 1 saucepan; 1 cotton tea strainer

■ Heat the wine in the saucepan until it begins to boil. Add the tea and allow to steep for 3 mins. Remove the tea leaves.

■ Sweeten to taste and serve.

■ Enjoy this winter drink piping hot, around the fire, after a meal with friends. In summer, serve iced as an aperitif. For this, use a light wine instead – Rivesaltes, Banyuls or Frontignan – and slightly sweeten, and store the preparation in the refrigerator.

■ *The marriage of tea and alcohol allows many combinations. Spiced, very fruity or floral teas go very well with the tannins in the wine. In a hot toddy, to enjoy when it's really cold, arak or white planters' rum will go well with vanilla or ginger teas. Once again chilled vodka with lightly spiced tea can be served between the starter and white meat courses.*

Index of recipes

MARIAGE FRÈRES

French Tea in Paris since 1854

TEA	TEA	TEA	TEA
MUSEUM	COUNTER	SALON	CUISINE

30 & 35 rue du Bourg-Tibourg
Le Marais Paris 4ᵉ

13 rue des Grands-Augustins
Rive Gauche Paris 6ᵉ

260 Faubourg Saint-Honoré
Étoile Paris 8ᵉ

Mail orders :

35 rue du Bourg-Tibourg   75004 Paris, France   Tel : +33(0)1 43 47 18 54 - Fax : +33(0)1 48 40 40 42

WWW.MARIAGEFRERES.COM

Acknowledgements

The discovery of tea flavours is a captivating taste
adventure to which Mariage Frères has been dedicated
for many generations.
Thanks to Philippe Langlois, Sébastien Delmas
and Daniel Milliner for understanding the spirit and
dressing the plates with such skill and enthusiasm.
Thanks to Laurent Sonnino for coordinating
the ingredients.
Thanks to Franck Desains for his infallible taste,
his expert eye and his enquiring and inspired mind.

Laurence du Tilly particularly thanks the following shops
for their invaluable help and kindness:

Christian Tortu, Home autour du Monde, L'île de la
Tortue, Les 2 mille feuilles, Kim et Garo, Madame Paris,
Mariage Frères, and No'.

The publisher thanks Carole Vernis for her valuable
contribution.

Photographic credits

Pages 2-3, 6, 7, 10: Walter-Donzel archives –
Mariage Frères museum.
Pages 4, 5: Hachette photo library.
Pages 8, 9: Mariage Frères archives
and packaging.

Managing editor of the French edition:
Brigitte Éveno
Managing editor of the English edition:
Juliette de Lavaur
Art direction: Marc Walter – China
Production: Gérard Lamarche
Translation: Lipsie
Manufacture: Caroline Artémon

©2002 HACHETTE LIVRE
(Hachette Pratique), for the French edition.
©2008 HACHETTE LIVRE
(Hachette Pratique), for the current edition.

Photo-engraving: Penez Éditions in Lille
Printed in Spain by Macrolibros
Registration of copyright: 01/2008
EAN: 300 201231746 3 – Ed.01